Python Programming

A Pragmatic Approach To Programming
Python for Total Beginners

Table of Contents

Introduction

Congratulations on purchasing *Python Programming* and thank you for doing so.

The following chapters will discuss what you need to know to get started writing the Python language. There are many different aspects of the Python code, and learning how to use all of it, and make it work for your needs can go a long way in the types of programs that you are able to write. Python coding is not meant to be difficult, it is designed to be used by beginners and advanced coders alike, so learning how to make your own codes with the Python language is going to be easier than you may think!

In this guidebook, we are going to take a look at many of the different things that you are able to do with the Python code. We will look at some of the basics to start, including why the Python language is so beneficial and so popular how to get this program set up on any computer and operating system that you want to use, and even some of the basics of most codes to help you get started with the compiler and more.

From there, we are going to move on to some of the special parts that you are able to work on when you are ready to write your codes. By the time we are done with this section, you will find that you can write some amazing codes, ones that make sure your program is up and running and ready to go. Some of the topics that we are going to look at in this chapter to help us get the best results with our coding and with learning how to use the different aspects of Python include exception handling, loops, decision control statements, the iterators, the generators, functions, variables, classes and more!

The main point of this guidebook is to help you go from a new coder, someone who may have never worked with any kind of coding in the past, who is ready to get started writing some of their own codes. If this is your goal, and you want to see how efficient and easy the Python code can be, make sure to check out this guidebook to help you get started.

Publications with the same subject flood the market and we appreciate you picked our book! Rest assured we strive to provide information in this book is as fun and informational. Have fun reading!

Chapter 1: What is Python and Why Is It So Popular?

Learning how to properly code can open up a lot of doors and opportunities for you. Some people like to learn how to code because they have a neat idea for a program or an app that you would like to use. Maybe you find that there is a better job and more that you can get if you learned a bit of coding and how to do this kind of work. A big promotion could be yours when you learn how to do this. Alternatively, maybe you just want to learn how to do this in order to impress your friends and family.

If you are exploring some of the options that are available when you pick out a coding language, you may want to consider going with Python. This is one of the most popular coding languages out there, mainly because it is available on any platform, and it is easy enough for beginners to learn, while still having all the power that your programs need.

The Python language is going to be a coding language that is designed for beginners and that better-versed in coding to write some of their own programs. It is open-sourced, which means that anyone is able to get it for their computer free of charge. And there is a dedicated group of developers who will work on updating and keeping the program working well, which can ensure that you are able to use it for all of your needs on a regular basis.

One concept to keep in your head here though is that, while the Python program is open source and free to use, there are some libraries and some extensions that are going to cost you. These work well with the Python program, and they are not a fraud. But with some of them, there was another company that developed a special program or special features, and they are selling this. If you want to have special features, you may need to pay. If you just want to use the basic functions that come with Python, which are usually plenty enough for most people, then you will be able to do it for free.

You will find that there are actually a lot of different benefits that you are able to get when you decide to work with the Python code. Some of the different benefits that you are able to get when you choose to write codes with the Python language include:

It is open-sourced. One thing that many people like about the Python code is that it is open-sourced. This means that even though someone is going through and working on the development and keeping it up to date, anyone is able to download it online and get all of the files that they need to go with it. Moreover, they are able to do this all for free. This means that if you already have a computer ready to go, you can get started with writing your own codes and working with the Python language, without having to pay for a thing.

It has a large library. We are going to spend quite a bit of time in this guidebook exploring some of the things that come with the Python library, and what you are able to enjoy while working on this kind of library. This is going to include the variables, the functions, the classes and objects, and many of the other things that you need to do while writing some of your own codes in this language.

The Python library, at least the standard version, is going to come with all of the things that you need to start writing your own codes, and it is free. However, if you want to do things that are a bit more technical, like machine learning, mathematics, graphs, and so on, there are other libraries that you will have to download at the same time. You can pick and choose whether these are important to you or not.

It is easy for beginners to use. As a beginner, you will find that the Python language is going to be one of the easiest languages for you to learn. Sure, you can learn any of the others and this is not meant to stop you from that. However, the beauty of this language is that it was designed to be easier, while still having a lot of power, for most beginners to use. If you have shied away from using some of the other coding languages because you didn't think they would work that well for you, or you were worried that they would be too hard, then you can rest easy knowing that the Python language is going to be easy to work with and any beginner can write their own codes in no time.

It has enough power for even advanced coders to work with While Python is often advertised as a language that is used by beginners because it is easy to read and the coding is not as complicated as with some of the other languages out there, don't let this fool you. Even coders who have been working with this for a long time, and who may have worked with a few other coding languages along the way have found a lot to enjoy when it comes to working with the Python code.

This is because the Python code is not just simple, it is also powerful. It is going to be able to keep up with a lot f the processing and a lot of the power that we see with some of the other coding languages but it is going to be easier to use, and it is written out in a way that makes it easier to read through as well. This is why this program is perfect for both beginners and those are more advanced coders to work with.

This coding language is also all about the classes and the objects. We will talk about this a bit more as we progress through this book, but this really makes coding easier for you. It ensures that when you call up a part of the code, as long as you name it and call it up in the right away, it is going to show up the way that you want. This may have been a struggle for some beginners in other coding languages, but this problem is solved with the help of the Python code.

It can work with other languages. Not only are you able to turn on the Python language and use all of the capabilities that come with it on your computer, but you can also combine it together with some other coding languages to really enhance some of the capabilities that you see on there. Python is able to do many different things, but there are a few points where it may fall a bit short, or that other coding languages are going to do better. Adding it together with one of these other coding languages can ensure that your program is written the way that you want.

Python is already being used in many different programs already. In fact, some of your favorite programs may already be using Python to help them run. You will find that Python is on many website and games and other common programs, and you may not have even noticed to begin. As we go through this guidebook, you may be pleasantly surprised at how great these programs work, even though many of the codes are simple to read and write.

It can be added to any computer. You will find that with some of the other coding languages out there, you will be limited based on the type of operating system that you use. This can be a pain because either you need to change up your operating system in order to use it, or you will not be capable to employ that coding language at all.

The neat thing about working in the Python language is that this is not a problem. You will not have to worry about what kind of operating system is already on your computer, and you will not be limited by the operating system at all, because Python is going to work on all of them. We will take a look at some of the different steps that you can take to make sure the Python files and program are ready to go on your computer.

There is a large community that you can work with. As you go through some of the coding that you want to work with, you may find that there is a part of the code that you are not sure about, an error that may come up, or you just need some help or another that you want to explore. If you were all on your own, this could be frustrating because you would be unsure of how to proceed.

The good news with this one is that the Python language is really popular throughout the world, which means that you will be able to find many other programmers, beginners and advanced, who will share their knowledge with you. You can ask questions, look at forums, or even watch some videos to learn what you need and to make sure that you will get the code written the way that you want.

There is just so much to love about the Python coding language. This guidebook is going to go over many of the different types of codes that you are able to write, and adding them together can ensure that you get the right code written for your needs, no matter what your goal for the end results are. Now that you know some of the benefits that come with this coding language, and how the Python language can work well with you, let's move on to installing the language, so we can really get some use out of writing our own codes!

Chapter 2: Setting Up the Python Program

Before we can start to work on some of the codes that you want to write with Python, we need to make sure that we are able to go through and actually download this program on our computer. You have to work with getting the files set up so that they work the right way, and unless you have certain versions of the Mac OS, you will need to install and download it first.

There are several places where you are able to get the Python program and make sure it is set up. One of the easiest to use though is www.python.org. This one is going to include all of the files that you need to make Python code writing work including the compiler, the interpreter, and the IDLE. You can choose to get the download from somewhere else if you would like, but double-check whether they have all three of the options above, or if you need to download some of your own before starting.

Python is able to work on any operating system that you want to use it with. With that in mind though, each type of operating system is going to have slightly different rules that you need to follow to get the system set up and ready to go. Some of the steps that you can take to get the Python program installed on any computer system that you would like.

Installing Python on Windows

The first operating system that we are going to look at here is the Windows system. This is a popular one for many programmers to use, but since it has its own coding language on it already, you will have to manually go through and install it on your system if you want to use Python. This one may take a few steps, but most of them are really easy and you can really get the Python code on your computer and working well in a few minutes once you get the hang of what you are doing.

Python is going to be just fine and will work the way that you want when you put it on a Windows computer. It is just not, there to start with because of Windows has its own coding program. All this means is that you need to take the steps to install it on your system to get it set up. Nevertheless, once you go through the installation steps that we will talk about in a minute, you will be able to enjoy the power and the ease of the Python language, even when you are on a Windows computer.

When you are ready to work with the Python language on your computer that has the Windows operating system, you will need to start out by going through and coming up with the right variables for the environment, so that you can actually run the scripts for Python from the command prompt that is there. The rest of the steps that you can follow to make sure that Python works well for your needs includes:

1. To help us get started with setting all of this up, go to the Python download page on their website and grab the installer that is listed for the Windows operating system. You can choose to go with any version of Python that you like but most coders like to work with the latest version of Python 3. The installer is going to give you the 32-bit version of Python, but you can change that based on the version of the operating system you are using with Windows.

2. Once you have the Windows installer from the Python website, it is time to right-click on it and select "Run as Administrator". As you do this, the system is going to provide you with two options that you need to decide on. For this, click on "Customize Installation."

3. On the screen that comes up next, make sure that all of the boxes that are under "Optional Features" have been selected and then click to go to the next page.

4. While you are still under the "Advanced Options", you will need to pick out the location where you would like to install Python. Once that folder is picked out, you can click to install. This takes a bit of time to install so have some patience with it. Once that install is done, you can close out of this part.

5. The next thing that we need to do is set up the PATH variable that works with this system so that you have all of the directories that will include packages and other components that are necessary to use later on. The way that you get all of this set up is going to use the steps below;

a. Open up your Control Panel. If you are not certain where this is, click on your taskbar and type in "Control Panel". Click on the little icon that shows up when you do this.

b. When you get the Control Panel to show up, you can check for "Environment" and then click on Edit the System Environment Variables. When this is done, you can then click on the button tagged "Environment Variables."

c. At this point, you can go to the section that is listed for User Variables. Either here you can decide to create a new PATH variable, or you can edit the PATH variable that is already in place.

d. If there is not a variable for PATH on the system as you are looking, then it is time for you to create your own. To do this, click on New. Give it a name, one that works for the PATH variable you are choosing, and then place it into the chosen directory. Click to closer yourself from the Control Panel at this time and then go to the next step.

6. When you get to this point, you can open up that Command Prompt again. You can do this by clicking on your Start Menu, then clicking on Windows System, and finally on Command Prompt. Type in the word "python". This will be enough to load up the interpreter of Python for you. \

Once you have been able to go through the steps above, which are actually faster than they may seem at the time, you will then be able to open up the Python language and use it in any manner that you would like in the Windows system.

You can even choose to get the interpreter and other parts of this code set up the way that you want them to and then write out codes when you are ready for that step.

Installing Python with the Linux operating system

The second type of operating system that you are able to work with is known as the Linux operating system, and this works well with the Python language as well. This operating system is really taking off, and it is able to work with a ton of different programs and systems that some of the others are not always able to handle. This makes it perfect for doing some of the coding that you want with the Python language, which is why we are going to take some time to explore how to download Python on this system.

The first thing to do here is to see if there is a variant of Python 3 is on your system. You can open up the command prompt on Linux and then run the following code:

$ python3 - - version

If you are on Ubuntu 16.10 or newer, then it is a simple process to install Python 3.6. You just need to use the following commands:

$ sudo apt-get update

$ sudo apt-get install Python3.6

If you are relying on an older version of Ubuntu or another version, then you may want to work with the deadsnakes PPA, or another tool, to help you download the Python 3.6 version. The code that you need to do this includes:

```
$ sudo apt-get install software-properties-common
$ sudo add-apt repository ppa:deadsnakes/ppa
# suoda apt-get update
$ sudo apt-get install python3.6
```

The good news that you are going to enjoy with this one is that if you choose to work with some of the other distributions that happen to come in the Linux family, it is possible that these systems already have Python 3 on them. It is all going to depend on the distribution that you use and whether they upgraded to have this or not.

If you find that this does not have the Python 3 on it as you would like or if the version of Python is not the one that you would like, you will just need to use the steps above in order to install the version of Python that you would like. Linux makes it pretty easy to work with Python and to get it all set up so you can start to write some of your own codes in no time.

Installing with the Mac OS X

The next option that we are going to focus on to make sure that we get the Python language installed on our computer is how to get it to work with the Mac operating system. It is likely that the Python 2 program is going to already be on this kind of operating system, so if you see that this is there, then there is not any more to do. Python 2 is just fine to work with and can help you to get things done. However, some people prefer to code with a more recent version of python rather than this one and will choose to work with one of the Python 3 options.

If you just want to check out which version of Python is on your computer, then you can open up your command prompt and type in "python – V". You will see the name of which version of Python 2 is there, and then you can choose if this is the one that you want or not.

If the Python 2 version is not up to date like you want, or you want to change to Python 3, which is possible as well with the Mac operating system, it is just going to take a few more steps to make this happen. Before we go through all of those steps though, we need to double-check whether Python 3 is present on the computer so you do not waste time. To do this, type in "python3 – V" and see if this gives you any results.

If you are not able to get results from this, and you want to get the Python 3 program set up on your Mac computer, make sure that you first uninstall the Python 2 version so that you do not get any confusion on the system. When that is off the computer, visit www.python.org as we discussed before and then pick out the version of Python that you would like to add to your computer.

Being able to run both the shell and the IDLE with the Python language is going to depend on which version of the program you decide to work with, as well as what preferences are there when you write out the code. The two biggest commands that you are going to use the most often to help make sure that the shell and IDLE applications start-up when you want will vary based on the version you use, and they are:

- For Python 2.X just type in "Idle"
- For Python 3.X, just type in "idle3"

As we talked about a bit before, when you take the time to download and install this Python 3 on the Mac operating system, you will need to install the IDLE so make sure that is there, and you can install it as a standard application inside of your Applications folder of course. To help you to start up this program using your desktop, you just need to go into the folder, double click on the application for the IDLE, and then you can wait for it to download.

Chapter 3: Some of the Basic Parts of the Python Code

Now that we have had some time to explore what the Python language is all about and some of the benefits that come with it, and we have an exceptional idea of some of the distinct means that you can install this language on your computer to use it, it is now time to learn more about the Python code. We are going to really take a look at some of the basic components that tend to show up with Python, and how you will be able to implement these into your code, especially with some of the more complicated ones that we will discuss later on in this guidebook.

There are so many types of codes that you are able to work with when it comes to Python, and it is all going to depend on the kind of program that you want to write out as well. Making sure that you know these basic parts though, and gaining a good understanding of how they work will make it easier for you to really write some of those more complicated codes later on. So, let us get started on some of the basics that come with the Python code.

Working on those keywords

The first basic part that we are going to explore when it comes with the Python code is the keywords. All coding languages are going to have keywords that they reserve to tell the compiler which action it should take. These are seen as special because they will be the commands that the compiler needs to follow along the way. Using them in the wrong way or in the wrong part of the code can result in the code not giving you the results that you want.

As you are working with the keywords with this kind of language, you must make sure that you are using them properly. You do not want to add them to the wrong part of the code. This often leads to an error message and can make things a bit tricky to work with. As you work with this code a bit more, you will learn what words are seen as keywords, and which ones you should only use for this, to get the best results.

These keywords are responsible for one thing, and that is to provide the compiler with the commands that it needs and helps the compiler know what it is supposed to do when you execute that command. These keywords are important to all of the codes that you decide to do, so when you are working on some Python code, double-check that you always put the keywords in the right place for your needs.

Naming your identifiers

We need to take a moment to take a look at some of the steps that you need to follow in order to properly name some of the identifiers that show up in your code. If you are not able to name these properly, you are going to find a lot of frustration with writing out some codes in this language. So, now we need to take a look at what these identifiers are all about and why they are important in your code.

As you work through Python, you may find that there are quite a few different identifiers that you can work with, even though they come under many different names including variables, entities, functions, and classes. Any time that you would like to name one of these identifiers though, be happy and relieved to know that the rules for doing so will be the same and will apply to all of them. Once we go through the rules for naming that are below, you will be able to name any identifier that you would like.

This brings us to the idea of naming the identifiers and learning which rules you have to follow to make this happen. First, you need to take some caution concerning the name that you give to the identifier. There are a ton of names that are available, and you can choose, for the most part, the name that you want. You get the choice of working with letters, both the uppercase and the lower case, and any number. The underscore symbol and any combination of the previous will work as well.

But there are a few restrictions to keep in mind with this as well when you start naming your identifier. First, it is not allowed for you to name any identifier with a number, and the name should not have any spaces that come with it. Naming the identifier, something like 5kids or 5 kids would get you an error, but naming it five kids or five kids would be just fine. Moreover, keep in mind that you should never use a keyword as the name of one of your identifiers or the compiler is going to get confused.

When you come up with the name that you want to give to that identifier, make sure that you remember what it is. It may follow all of the rules that you need, but if you are not able to remember the name when it is time to execute the code or pull out that identifier later on, then there can be some issues. If you call it the wrong thing or you spell it differently, then there could be an error or the compiler is going to get confused.

With that in mind, if you pick a name that makes sense for the identifier that you are working with, and you make sure to follow the rules that you talked about above, then you are going to be just fine and the code will work the way that you would like.

Looking at the control flow

The control flow in this language can be important. This control flow is there to ensure that you wrote out the code the proper way. There are some types of strings in your code that you may want to write out so that the compiler can read them the right way. But if you write out the string in the wrong manner, you are going to end up with errors in the system. We will take a look at many codes int his guidebook that follows the right control flow for this language, which can make it easier to know what you need to get done and how you can write out codes in this language.

A word about statements

The next thing that we need to explore on our list is known as the statements. Statements are just sentences that show up in Python that you would like to have on the screen when the code executes. They are just strings of code that you will write out, and that you tell the compiler to list out on the screen. When you tell the compiler the instructions that you want it to be able to work on, you will find that those are going to be some of the statements in your code.

When it comes to the statements, as long as you are able to write them out in the proper manner, the compiler will be able to read them and will ensure that you get the message that you want to show up on the screen. Remember that you can make these statements either long or short, depending on what works for the code that you will work on. You will see many statements that show up in the codes that you write, including some of the examples that we list out in this guidebook.

Comments and how they work

Comments are another part of the code that you need to learn, and it is likely that you will see quite a few of these, especially at the beginning of any code that we decide to work with. There are going to be some times when you are writing out code inside of this language, and it seems like it is a favorable idea to include a note or some kind of explanation about what is happening in the code. You are able to do this with the help of a comment.

These comments can be nice because you can add them in so that someone reading through the code knows what is going on, but you will not see any effect with your program. It keeps things organized; helps to explain some of the things that you have going on in the code, and can make things easier, without any issues to how well your code is working.

As a programmer, you will see that it can be easy to add in these comments, and you can add in as many as you would like. To make your own comment in Python, you just need to add in "#" and then follow it with the statement that you want to have there. This sign is enough to tell the compiler that you are creating your own comment, and the compiler will see it, and avoid working on the comment at all, automatically skipping to the next part of the code.

You get the choice to add as many of these comments as you would like to the codes that you decide, as long as they are not just there to take up room and actually explain what is going to in that part of the code. You could have lines and lines of code if you would like, though most coders try to avoid this to keep the program working smoothly and to make it easier to read through any code that they write. But technically, as long as you have that symbol in front of your statement, it is possible to add in as many of these comments as you would like, and the compiler will know that it should not read that and should go to the next part of the code.

The variables

We also need to take a moment to talk about variables and how they are an important part of the Python code you are writing. They are going to be more common than you may originally think. The main reason that we need to take a look at the variables is that they are responsible for storing different values that you place inside of your code, and will make sure that any line of code that you decide to write is going to be organized, easy to read and will execute the way that you would like.

The best part is that they are simple to work with. All that you need to do in order to make sure that a value is correctly assigned to a variable is to add in an equal sign between the value and the variable, and the compiler will be able to do the rest for you. You can choose any value to go with your variable, just make sure that the equal sign is in place.

Another thing that is possible to do with the help of the variable is assigned more than one value to each variable. If you just add in the equal sign on both of these values and get them to go back to the variables you want to work with. If you take a look down at some of the different codes that we have written out and examples that are in this guidebook, you will find that there are many variables in place with them.

Ending with the operators

The final basic part of the Python code that we are going to take a look at here is known as the operators. These are going to be simple, and there are a lot of different operators out there that you are able to work with based on what kind of code. You can work with some that help you to add a few parts of your code together. You can work with some that will help you to assign names to your identifiers as we talked about before, and some that help to decide if a part of the code is considered true or false. Think of all the possibilities that you can do with these operators once you learn how to use them properly?

As you take a look through some of the different codes that we will work on in this guidebook, many different operators are going to show up. Moreover, often you will use them without even realizing what you are doing at the time or realizing that you are working with the operators. But it would be almost impossible to do any kind of coding if you were not able to add in the operators along with some of the other parts.

These are just a few of the basic parts that you are able to work on when it comes to creating your own codes in Python. These may seem simple, and you may wonder why you would need to use these in the first place, but there are so many times that you are going to see these basics show up in the code that you are trying to write, and having a strong working knowledge of them can make coding in Python so much easier.

Chapter 4: What are the Variables in Python?

The first topic that we are going to take a look at is the Python variables. We looked at this a bit before, but we need to go into more detail to see exactly why these variables are so important, and why they are going to help our code to work the way that we want. These variables are basically going to be anything that is able to hold a value, a value that is able to change. To keep it simple, the variable is just going to be a box that is able to hold onto things in the code. This is important because they will be able to pull out a saved space that is in your memory on the computer so that you are able to pull it out and use it in the code as needed.

These variables are going to be good for us to learn because you can store them into the memory of the code, and you are able to ask the compiler to pull these out when they are needed. This means that the variables that you decide to create are going to be placed throughout the memory, where there is room, on your computer, and if they are assigned properly, you will be able to find the variables that you need at the right time. Hinged on the type of data that you are aiming to do with, the variable is going to help the compiler know where to store the information so you can find it later.

Now that we have some idea of how the variables are going to work, and some of the importance that comes with it, let us look at how to assign values to the variables, and some more of the neat things that we are able to do when it comes to the variables in the Python code.

How to assign a value to the variable

To make sure that we are able to get our variable to act the way that we want, it is important to assign at least one value over to the variable. Without a value, and if you miss this step, then you will end up saving something in the memory like normal, but space is going to be empty, and when the compiler does its work, it won't pull up anything when the code runes. If the variable is taken care of the way that it should, and you assign a value to it, and sometimes even more than one value to the same variable, then the memory will have something saved in that spot and the code will work properly.

As we go through and work on these variables, you are going to find that the process is going to include three options that are available to work with. Each of these can be useful, and the method that you pick often depends on what you want to have happened inside the code. The three types of variables that you are going to be able to pick out from include:

- Float: this would include numbers like 3.14 and so on.
- String: this is going to be like a statement where you could write out something like "Thank you for visiting my page!" or another similar phrase.

- Whole number: this would be any of the other numbers that you would use that do not have a decimal point.

When you are working with variables in your code, you need to remember that you do not need to take the time to make a declaration to save up this spot in the memory. This is automatically going to happen once you assign a rate over to the variable using the match a sign. If you want to check that this is going to happen, just look to see that you added that equal sign in and everything is going to work.

Assigning a value over to your variable is pretty easy. Some examples of how you can do this in your code would include the following:

x = 12   *#this is an example of an integer assignment*

pi = 3.14   *#this is an example of a floating point assignment*

customer name = John Doe   *#this is an example of a string assignment*

This is just part of the equation and only one of the options that you are able to do with this. We also mentioned for a bit in this chapter how it is possible to assign two or more values to the same variable if you would like. This may not happen as often as you would see with just having one variable to one value, but there may be certain instances in your code where you will need to make sure that two values are stored in the same place in the computer memory, and so you will assign these two values to the same variable.

This means that we need to learn how to make this happen. To assign two values to the same variable, you will need to work with pretty much the same steps that we talked about above. You just need to make sure that there are equal signs between each value that attaches them back to the variable that you are working on as well. It is as simple as that.

Let us take a look at how to make this happen. A good example would be something like a = b = c = 1 to show the compiler that all three of those values are going to go back to the variables. You can also choose to work with something like 1 = b = 2 to show that there are two values that go with that particular variable. You can choose which of these two methods works best for what you want to do there.

The one thing that we need to remember when it comes to doing with these variables is that it needs to be given a value. A variable without a value is going to be worthless as it means nothing will happen at that point in the code. When this is done, and the variable has at least one value that has been attached back to it, you know that the piece of memory that the variable is holding has been filled and that the compiler will know how to call back the value when the program is up and running.

Chapter 5: Working with Functions

Now that we have had a chance to learn about the variables and how they store some values in the memory of the computer for us, it is now time to look a bit more at some other topics that are going to help us get more done in this code. For this part, we are going to take a look at functions, because this is something that will be mentioned quite a bit through this guidebook. Let us dive right into the functions and learn how to make these works in the proper manner inside our Python code.

To start out this topic, we are going to look at the functions and what they are all about. These functions are going to be known for being a set of expressions, which is sometimes called the statements as well. These can come in two main methods either with a name, or they are going to be kept anonymous based on how you want to use them. They are going to be some of the first-class objects that you add into the code, which means that there won't already be a lot of restrictions on how you are able to use them in your code.

With these functions, you will find that you can use them in a similar manner that values in the code are used, even like the strings and the numbers, and they will have some attributes that we need to lookout. You can bring out the attributes using the dir prefix in the code.

Functions are special because they can be very diversified, and they will show up in many different parts of the code that you are writing. Moreover, they are going to bring in many attributes that you are able to bring into the code as you create the functions. A few of the choices that are available to use when you create some of these functions include:

- __doc__: This is going to return the docstring of the function that you are requesting.
- Func_default: This one is going to return a tuple of the values of your default argument.
- Func_globals: This one will return a reference that points to the dictionary holding the global variables for that function.
- Func_dict: This one is responsible for returning the namespace that will support the attributes for all your arbitrary functions.
- Func_closure: This will return to you a tuple of all the cells that hold the restrained for the complimentary variables inside of the function.

There are different things that you can do with your functions, such as passing it as an argument over to one of your other functions if you need. Any function that is able to take on a new one as the argument will be considered the higher-order function in the code. These are good to learn because they are important to your code as you move.

Chapter 6: Exception Handling in Python

There are many cool things that you are able to do when you work on the Python coding language. Some of them are going to be relatively simple and will help you to just write out some simple statements on the screen, and others are going to take it a bit farther and try to write out full codes and more, and even games and other programs while you use many different techniques.

With this in mind, we are going to move on to a look at exception handling with the help of Python. As you start to create some of the codes that you would like to work on in Python, you are going to find that there are some exceptions that can show up. Sometimes these are exceptions that the program is going to automatically recognize and will bring up for you, and other times you will be able to create on your own in order to make a particular program work. Any of them that the code ends up showing to you automatically are going to be found in the Python library, so you can go ahead and peruse that if you are interested in learning more.

For example, let us say that the user gets to a certain part of your code and they want to start dividing by zero. This is something that the Python language, as well as many of the other coding languages out there, are not going to allow to happen. We will look at how this exception is going to look in the code, as well as some of the things that you can do to change up the exception and make sure that it makes sense and actually goes along with your code.

In addition to some of the automatic exceptions that your code is going to start bringing up for you, it is possible that you can raise some of your own. This is going to depend on the kind of code that you are trying to write. If there is something within the program that you would like to limit, or you want to make sure that the user is not able to do something, then this is when you would want to add in the exception.

Now, we need to focus on the automatic exceptions, the ones that the program already recognizes on its own. If the user end sup doing one of these things that the program will not allow, the exception will be raised and the program is not going to let it all finish. This could be something like calling up the wrong name of a function, dividing by zero, and so on.

As a programmer, it is important that you have a good idea of some of the different exceptions that are going to show up in your code, and looking through the Python library is going to help you with this. This helps you to know how to write out each part of the code and can help you be prepared for what can turn up in the code as well. A few of the most common exceptions that are going to show up in the Python code, along with some of their keywords, will include the following:

1. Finally: This is going to be the action that you want to put in because it helps to do any cleanup actions that need to be done in the code, whether the exception is brought up in this particular code or not.

2. Assert: This is a condition that will make sure that the exception is triggered inside of the code.

3. Raise: This raise command is a good one to learn about because it is going to help you to manually get an exception raised inside of your code if you want to create your own.

4. Try or except: This option is going to be when you want to be able to see whether a block of code is going to work, and then that code is recovered thanks to the exceptions. The exceptions that save the code can either by ones that you raise or by ones that the Python code automatically raises for you.

How to raise these exceptions in your code:

The first thing that we need to take a look at here is the idea of how you would be able to use these exceptions that can come up in your code, especially when they are automatic exceptions. When these exceptions end up in your code, it is important for you as the programmer to be prepared and to know what you are able to do with some of the codings in order to get past them and to make them even easier to understand.

Let us say that you are designing your own code, and you notice that there is a place where the user could potentially have an exception show up. You can then take a look at any notice that the compiler is going to bring up when you use the code, and see if it is raising this kind of exception. This shows up because your program has had a chance to look through the code, it seems that this problem is there, and now it wants to know what you would like to have done.

The good news here is that often, the issues that raise the exceptions that are automatic are pretty easy for you to fix. For example, you or the user may try to bring up a file, and it was either given the wrong name or when you went to search for it, you typed in the wrong name. The compiler is not going to be able to find a match when you do this, and that is when it raises an exception. The program was able to look through the code and sees that there is nothing it can do to help.

Now, this can seem like a complicated process to work within your code, but it does have many benefits. A good way to start to see how these exceptions are going to work is to take some time and make our own example. We can then see what will happen with our compiler, and how it can raise an exception when we set it all up. An example of a code that you can type into the compiler to make this happen includes:

$x = 10$

$y = 10$

result = x/y #trying to divide by zero

print(result)

The output that you are going to get when you try to get the interpreter to go through this code would be:

>>>

Traceback (most recent call last):

    File "D: \Python34\tt.py", line 3, in <module>

    result = x/y

ZeroDivisionError: division by zero

>>>

When you have had some time to put this example into your compiler, you will see that there is an error or an exception is raised, because the user has gone through the code and is trying to divide by zero, which is not allowed with this kind of coding.

As a programmer, you have a choice now. You can definitely just leave the code like this and get the error message above. However, when your user comes on, looks at this, and sees that long and messy error message, how likely is it that they will have any idea what is going on? They will probably not understand what is going on, and it will just look like a mess to them. This is why we need to take this a step further and work on creating a code that is easier to read and to change up the message that comes up when you do the exception handling.

A better idea is to look at some of the different options that you can add to your code to help prevent some of the mess from before. You want to make sure that the user understands why this exception is being raised, rather than leaving them confused in the process. A different way that you can write out this code to make sure that everyone is on the same page includes:

```
x = 10
y = 0
result = 0
try:
        result = x/y
        print(result)
except ZeroDivisionError:
        print("You are trying to divide by zero.")
```

If you take some time to type this into the compiler and then compare to the answer that we got above, you will find that the error message that shows up is going to be a lot easier to read, and the user will actually understand what they did wrong. They can look at this message, and then go back through and make the changes that are needed. You do not have to add in this, but when it comes to making an easily usable code, it is a nice addition to have.

Defining an exception that is all your own.

In the work that we did above, we were able to see how to handle some of the exceptions that are going to come up because they are found in the Python library. This is a good way to gain some familiarity with the idea of exceptions and will help you to change it up and make the messages easier to work with if you would like, rather than leaving it as a string of numbers and letters that you will struggle with, much less your user.

Now we need to take it to the next level and look at how you are able to take something that would normally be fine in the code, and turn it into an exception. This can be done in a lot of games that you would like to make, or a few other examples where you want to limit what the user is able to do at that particular time.

Maybe you decide to work on some kind of code and you want to make sure that only certain letters or certain numbers, or a certain number of times that they can try something out at this point. Often games or forms are going to need to use this to its advantage. The way that you raise an exception is going to depend on the kind of programming that you are trying to create, but the same basic ideas are going to apply.

When you do these kinds of exceptions, you will find that they are going to be really unique to the type of code that you are writing. If you did not add in the right coding for this, then the compiler will not recognize that there is a problem, and it will continue to run the program the way that it wants, rather than the way that you want it designed. The neat thing here is that you are able to add in any kind of exception that you would like here and write out any message, and it is going to follow an idea that is similar to what we did in the other section.

Let us break this down a bit and look at some of the steps that you can take in order to really write out your own exceptions, along with the messages that go with them, in the code you are doing:

```
class CustomException(Exception):
def_init_(self, value):
        self.parameter = value
def_str_(self):
        return repr(self.parameter)


try:
        raise CustomException("This is a CustomError!")
except CustomException as ex:
        print("Caught:", ex.parameter)
```

When you finish this particular code, you are done successfully adding in your own exception. When someone does raise this exception, the message "Caught: This is a CustomError!" will come up on the screen. You can always change the message to show whatever you would like, but this was there as a placeholder to show what we are doing. Take a moment here to add this to the compiler and see what happens.

Exception handling is something that you will work with a lot more as you start to write out some more advanced codes in Python. There are a lot of times that you will work either with the exceptions that are recognized by the program or ones that you want to bring up for the code that you are writing in particular. Working with some of the codes that we bring up in this chapter will help you to deal with these exceptions and will ensure that you are able to make them look good to the user. Make sure to try a few of these codes in your compiler to ensure that you get some practice with these exceptions and that you are able to get a good idea of how these exceptions are supposed to work.

Chapter 7: The Elif or Conditional Statements

While it would be nice to set, up a program and get it to behave in the manner that we want all of the time. We would love to be able to guess all of the answers that someone is going to give us when they use the program, but in many cases, this is going to be impossible. For example, if you have a code that asks the user what their favorite color is, it is going to take forever to write out a code that has all of the colors of the world, and it is likely that you would miss some. Plus, that would take a long time and make the code look messy.

When you want to write out a code that is able to make decisions for you, based on some of the conditions that you set, then it is time to bring in the conditional statements, also known as the decision control statements. Pretty much any time that you are going to allow the user to add in an answer on their own, rather than listing out a menu with options for them, you will need to use these decision control statements so that the computer starts to know what steps you want it to take based on your conditions.

The first thing that we need to take a look at is the fact that there are going to be three different types of conditional statements. These include the if statement, the if else statement, and the elif statement. We will take a look at each of these to learn how they work, and when you may want to use them to make your code work properly.

The first of the conditional statements we are going to take a look at is known as the if statement. This one is pretty simple, and there may not be a ton of chances to use it in your code. But it still does work in the code, and can be a great way to learn more about these conditional statements.

The if the statement is going to rely on the idea that the answer the user gives is either true or false. The answer matches up with the conditions that you set, or it does not. This does not mean that the answer the user gives is wrong. It just means that it does not match up with the conditions that you have set up there at all and that is how the computer sees it. If the user puts in an answer that the computer agrees with, then they are going to get the information that you added into the code. But if the compiler sees the answer and determines it is false, then the program is going to end because it simply doesn't really know what it is supposed to do next (unless you added in more to handle this).

To get a better idea of how the if the statement is going to look, and how it is able to work, inside of your code, take a look at an example of the if statement that we have below:

```
age = int(input("Enter your age:"))
if (age <=18):
        print("You are not eligible for voting, try next election!")
print("Program ends")
```

Let us explore what is going to happen with this code when you put it into your program. If the user comes to the program and puts that they are younger than 18, then there will be a message that shows up on the screen. In this case, the message is going to say "You are not eligible for voting, try next election!" Then the program, as it is, is going to end. However, what will happen to this code if the user puts in some age that is 18 or above?

With the if statement, nothing will happen if the user says that their age is above 18. The if statement just has one option and will focus on whether the answer that the user provides is going to match up with the conditions that you set with your code. The user has to put in that they are under the age of 18 with the if statement in this situation or you will not be adept to get the program to happen again.

As you can imagine when you are working on this, there could be a few problems that arise when you try to use them if statement in some of the codes that you write. Your goal with the example above is not to force the user to put in a certain age to make the program work. You want them to put in any age that they actually are at the time. Their age is not wrong, and it is not true or false, so there are some limitations to what you are able to do with the if statements. This is why the if-else statements, as well as the elif statements that we will talk about in a minute, are going to be important to work with as well.

First, we are going to look at the if-else statements. These are going to follow the same kind of idea as we find with the if statements above, but it helps to solve some of the problems that you may encounter, and will make it easier to get the right response based on the input from the user. This statement is going to help your user to get an answer, no matter what age group they decide to put into the program.

Going from the idea that we talked about above, you will want to allow the user to come in and input any age that they want into the system. When you use the if-else statement, you can separate the ages based on those who are under 18, and those who are 18 and above, and then have responses show up in the program for each one. Let us peek at an instance that shows us how these if-else statements are going to work:

age = int(input("Enter your age:"))
if (age <=18):

     print("You are not eligible for voting, try next election!")
else

     print("Congratulations! You are eligible to vote. Check out your local polling station to find out more information!)
print("Program ends")

As you can see, this really helps to add some more options to your code and will ensure that you get an answer no matter what results the user gives to you. You can also change up the message to say anything that you want, but the same idea will be used no matter the answer that the user gives.

You have the option to add in some more possibilities to this. You are not limited to just two options as we have above. If this works for your program, that is just fine to use. However, if you need to use more than these two options, you can expand out this as well. For example, take the option above and expand it to have several different age groups. Maybe you want to have different options come for those who are under 18, those that are between the ages of 18 and 30, and those who are over the age of 30. You can separate it out in that way and when the program gets the answer from the user, it will execute the part that you want.

You are not limited to this one though. There are many examples of how the if-else statement is going to be able to add in some strength to the types of programs you are writing. Let us say that you wish to write out a program that allows the user to pick out the color that is their favorite. You may go through the program and list out six colors with responses to it. The user may pick one of those six colors, or they may pick something completely different.

If the user picks out a color that is on your list, then they are going to get the statement or the result that you have listed with it. However, if they pick out a different color that is on the list (which is possible because it would be very hard to list out all of the colors in the world), then the catchall or the final message is going to show up.

This catch-all, or the "else" part of the code, is something that is so important and you need to make sure to add it into this code if you are working with an if-else statement. In many cases of using these conditional statements, it is going to be impossible to think up all of the answers that someone is going to put in, and this can take forever even if you try. The catch-all part of this is going to catch any answer that is put in and does not match with the ones that you have listed out earlier in the code.

The if-else statement is a great one to learn how to use because it helps you to handle a situation where the user is going to have many different potential answers, and you want to make sure you get a response for all of them. If you do not have a statement to handle any of the cases you missed with answers from the user, then the else part of the statement will handle it for you and can make the code run smoothly.

Now that we have had a chance to work with the if statement and with the if-else statement, it is time to move on to what is known as the elif statements. This is going to take the ideas that we have been talking about with the other two conditional statements and bring it a bit further. This one is also going to follow the idea of a menu option. The user will be given a menu of what they want to pick from, and then when they make a choice, your program will execute the kind of statement that you want.

There are many codes that are going to utilize the elif statement, and it just depends on what you are trying to write. One good example of when you are going to see the elif statement is during a game when a menu style of choices comes up and you have to make a decision based on that information. These statements are going to be used if you want to provide more options than one or two back over to your user.

With the elif statement, you do have some freedom. You can choose to have as many of these statements present in the code as you want, as long as you write out the code in the proper manner and you make sure that you add in the right function to go along with them. In addition, having too many of these could mean that you have a complicated code that is a bit harder to write out than others, but if it works well for your program, then it is just fine to add in as many as you would like.

To better, understand how these elif statements are going to work, here is a good example of the syntax that comes with these statements:

if expression1:

statement(s)

elif expression2:

statement(s)

elif expression3:

statement(s)

else:

statement(s)

The above is going to just contain the syntax that you will need to use when you want to create your own elif statement in your code. You are able to add onto this or take away based on how many options you would like to provide to your user. Just take the syntax then, and add in the information that should go with each part.

As you get a chance to read through this syntax and see what is there, notice that there is a nice else statement that comes at the end, similar to what we saw with the if-else statement before. Just like before, you need to make sure that this is added into the code at the very end. It is critical to put that in so that it is able to get all of the answers that the user wants that do not fit with the options you list above.

What we looked at above is just the syntax that comes with the elif statements, but there is so much that you are able to do with this. Now that we have a better idea of how the syntax for the elif statement is supposed to look, let's go through and add in an example to see what it would look like, or similar to, when you use it inside of your own code:

Print("Let's enjoy a Pizza! Ok, let's go inside Pizzahut!")
print("Waiter, Please select Pizza of your choice from the menu")

```
pizzachoice = int(input("Please enter your choice of Pizza:"))
if pizzachoice == 1:
        print('I want to enjoy a pizza napoletana')
elif pizzachoice == 2:
        print('I want to enjoy a pizza rustica')
elif pizzachoice == 3:
        print('I want to enjoy a pizza capricciosa')
else:
        print("Sorry, I do not want any of the listed pizza's; please bring a Coca
Cola for me.")
```

Now the user is going to be able to go through and make the choices that they want and they will get the right option to meet with them. For example, if they want to go with the pizza rustica, they will pick the number 2. If they want to have, just a drink rather than one of the other choices above, they can do that too. While we did use the example of pizza in here, there are many other things that you can do with it, so pretty much if you want your user to have some options, you would use the syntax that is above and then fills in the options that work the best for you.

As we took some time to discuss in this guidebook, working with the conditional statements can add in a lot of great power to the codes that you are trying to write. The reason for this is that they do add in some more power than a few of the other options that we have talked about so far in this guidebook, helps the program to make decisions on its own, and can really change the game when working on your own codes.

To make sure that you get a good understanding of how to work with the conditional statements, all three of them, make sure to open up your compiler and add some of the codes into it. This gives you some practice with writing these and ensures that you can see how each one is similar and how each one is different.

Chapter 8: What are Loops and How Can They Help My Code?

There are many different things that you are able to do when it comes to working with the Python language. In addition, the next thing that we are going to explore and learn how to use are the loops. These loops are very important when you are writing your code and the amount of time that you are able to save when using it is going to make things so much easier in the long run. Loops help to clean up the program and can fit a lot of information in just a few lines of code, helping to make your life easier.

If you are working on any kind of code where you need the compiler to go through and re-read the same part more than one time, usually at least a few times, then the loops are going to be helpful. We will take a look at how you are able to do this, without having to re-write the same line or lines of code a bunch of times.

Sure, you can definitely go through and code all that you want without these loops. You can just rewrite all of the lines repeatedly. This may not seem like a big deal if you just need it to repeat two or three times. However, what if the code could potentially repeat itself a hundred times or more? You can do this with the loop and it really isolates takes a lesser line of code, rather than potentially hundreds if you do not use the loop.

There are many examples of working with these loops in your code. Let us say that you are working on some kind of code where you want it to list out all of the numbers from one to ten but you do not want to waste your time writing out all of the lines of code to make this happen. The loop is going to be able to help you get it all done without having to write so much or making the code into a big mess in the process.

The process of working with these loops is going to be so much easier than it sounds in the beginning, and it will not take long before you start to really appreciate them in your own code. They are there to talk with the compiler and tell it that instead of moving on to the next part; it needs to repeat that certain part of code until some conditions are met. You will be the one to determine what conditions the compiler needs to meet before it moves on from the loop. To help us get a better understanding of how these loops work, we will take a look at a few examples of loops that you are able to work with.

This brings us to the next point. When you are writing out the loops, you need to make sure that there is always a condition set up. If you forget to put in this condition or assume that you do not really need one, then your program is not going to work right. If everything else is set up properly, but the condition is missing, the compiler will continue to re-read the same part of code repeatedly, with no idea about when it should start. Your program will effectively be frozen at that point.

Think about how much space and time this is going to save you. When you work with some of the previous examples of coding that we have talked about, you would be responsible for writing out each line of code that you need. If you need to have the program count from one to ten, then you would have to repeat the code in this manner. However, since you are basically doing the same thing, and you just want the compiler to repeat the same thing, you will be able to work with the loop in order to make this happen.

This is one of the best things when it comes to learning how to use a loop. You no longer have to write it all out and can easily combine a lot of lines of code into just a few, and make sure that the right words are placed into the code so that the compiler knows how many times you want it to go through that part of the code. With one or two lines of code, the loops can get a ton of coding done in the process for you.

As you work through your Python language, you will find that there are actually quite a few loops that are available for you to try out, based on what kind of program you would like to write. The three main types that we are going to take a look at including the nested loop, the while loop, and the for a loop. Let us take a look at how these each work, how they are similar, and some of the differences that come with them.

What is the while loop

Out of the three-loop types that we talked about above, we are going to start our study off with the while loop. This type of loop is one that you will choose any time that you know how many iterations of the cycle that you want the code to go through and you want to make sure the compiler reads through at least that many times. If you want to make sure that the compiler reads through the loop at least one time, for example, then you will want to work with the while loop to make this happen.

With the while loop, your goal is not to make the code go through its cycle an indefinite amount of times, but you do want to make sure that it goes through for a specific number of times. If you are counting from one to ten, you want to make sure it goes through the loop ten times to be right. With this option, the loop is going to go through at least one time and then check to see if the conditions are met or not. Therefore, it will put up the number one, then check its conditions and put up number two, and so on until it sees where it is.

To give us a little bit better of an understanding on how these loops work, let us take a glimpse at a few sample codes of the while loop and see what happens:

counter = 1

while(counter <= 3):

    principal = int(input("Enter the principal amount:"))

    numberofyeras = int(input("Enter the number of years:"))

```
rateofinterest = float(input("Enter the rate of interest:"))

simpleinterest = principal * numberofyears * rateofinterest/100

print("Simple interest = %.2f" %simpleinterest)

#increase the counter by 1

counter = counter + 1

print("You have calculated simple interest for 3 time!")
```

Now that we have a better idea of what the while loop is going to look like, make sure to stop here and add the code above into your compiler and then let it execute. When this one is done, the output is going to be set up in a way that the user is able to place in any information that they want into this program. Once that is done, the program is going to go through the computations necessary, and then can see the interest rates, the final amounts, and more based on the numbers that your user, or yourself, decided to add into the system.

With the example that we used above, we made it so that the while loop would go through three times. This means that the user is allowed to put in the input of their choice three times, and then this part of the program will be done. As the programmer, you are able to go through and make some changes, adding in more loops, for example, to ensure that this program works the way that you want it to work.

Moving on to the for loop

Another option that you are able to work with when it comes to the idea of loops in Python is known as the for a loop. The for loop is going to work in a lot of different situations, especially when you just want the program to repeat as many times as it needs to in order to get the work done. This for loop is more common to see because it can often cover a lot of the same things that the while loop can, and it is seen as the more traditional form of this process.

With the for loop, you will have it set up so that the user isn't the one who goes in and gives the program information that determines when the loop will stop. Instead, the for loop is set up to go over the iteration in the order that things show up inside your statement, and then this information is going to show up on your screen. There is not any need for input from an outside force or user, at least until it reaches the end. An example of the code that you can use to work on a for loop includes:

 # Measure some strings:
words = ['apple', 'mango', 'banana', 'orange']
for w in words:
print(w, len(w))

If you decide to work with the example that we have of a for loop above, you can take a moment to type it into your compiler and see what shows up on the screen when this executes. When you do this, the four fruits are going to show up on the screen, appearing in the same order that they are written out above. You do have the choice to change them up in terms of the order or how many are there, but once they are placed into the code, they are going to stay there, and changes are not allowed.

What the nested loop is all about

Now that we have had a chance to look at the while loop and the loop, it is time to work on the third and final loop known as the nested loop. This one is a bit different compared to the other two, but you will find that there can be a lot of situations where this loop is going to be the most helpful. When you do work with the nested loop, you are going to put one loop in with another loop, and then you will allow both of these loops to run together until they are done with their job.

This may seem like a strange thing to add to your code, but there are actually a lot of times when this is going to work out well with the code that you are trying to write. For example, you may decide that a game or another program you are writing needs something like a multiplication table. You can use the idea of the nested loop in order to make sure the code writes out the whole table going from one to ten and includes all of the answers that you need to have to go with each part.

This would be a huge amount of code if you wrote out each line to tell the program how to behave. And you can certainly do that if you want to waste some time practicing your code writing. However, a better method to use to make this work, a way that would get it done in relatively few lines of code and save you,

time includes the following:

#write a multiplication table from 1 to 10

For x in xrange(1, 11):

    For y in xrange(1, 11):

    Print '%d = %d' % (x, y, x*x)

When you got the output of this program, it is going to look similar to this:

1*1 = 1

1*2 = 2

1*3 = 3

1*4 = 4

All the way, up to 1*10 = 2

Then it would move on to do the table by twos such as this:

2*1 =2

2*2 = 4

And so on until you end up with 10*10 = 100 as your final spot in the sequence.

Go ahead, put this into the compiler, and see what happens. You will simply have four lines of code, and end up with a whole multiplication table that shows up on your program. Think of how many lines of code you would have to scribble out to get this table the traditional way that you did before? This table only took a few lines to accomplish, which shows how powerful and great the nested loop can be.

As you can see, there are many times when you may decide to use these loops and see how well they are able to fit into your code. There are many times when you will need to make a loop and add it to the code in order to get more things done, without a mess and without having to use a lot of code writing in the process. Try out some of the codes in this chapter and see how to work with the loops and how you can add this into your code.

Chapter 9: Classes and Objects in Python

One of the things that you are going to enjoy when it comes to using the Python language is that it is made up of classes and objects. We are going to get into more details about what all of this means and why this is important, but remember that this is going to really help you to keep things organized, and can keep your code easier to write out.

Classes and objects are important to learn how to work with because inside of the code, they are going to be there to ensure you can sort through all of the different parts found in the code. They are also going to make sure that when you save any of the parts of your code, you will be able to find them in the right spot again, without any movement when it is time to get the code to execute the code when it is time.

The objects are important as well because they will be what defines the different parts of the code, which helps you and the person using the code understand what is being done there. You still need to work with the classes as well because the class is in charge of holding onto the classes. With that introduction in mind, it is time for us to learn how to create our own objects and classes, and how to make these work together.

Creating a class in Python

The first thing that we need to take a look at is how to create one of the classes in the Python language. This is not something that the Python language is going to be able to do for you so you need to make sure you learn how to do it. Once you can create your own classes, you will be able to use them to organize the code and will ensure that none of the objects will end up lost in the process. The best way to get the classes made though is to make sure that you use the right keywords, and then come up with the name of the class.

The neat thing about working with this one is that you will gain a bit of freedom when you use this one. You can give the class that you create any kind of name that you would like. However, the thing for you to keep in mind with doing this is that the name needs to come after the keyword. It can also help you to come up with a name for the class that you are able to remember later when you need to pull that class up.

After you have been able to name a particular class that you are working on, then it is time to work with the subclass that comes with it. This subclass is going to be easy to find because it is going to be found inside the parenthesis of the code after the name of the class. Your job here is to make sure that when you are naming the subclass you add it to the parenthesis, and then add in a semicolon as well. While your code will work just fine without the semicolon, using it is considered part of the proper coding protocol.

If you are just starting out with the idea of the classes and objects, you may worry that creating one of these classes is going to be hard. You are responsible for creating pretty much a container that will help hold onto many different objects. How are you going to write in some code that helps to get all of this done and working together

This may seem complicated, but like with some of the other codes that are in this guidebook, once we look at some of the examples of how to do this, you will be able to see some great results and will find it is not as complicated as it seems. Let us examine at an example of the syntax that you are able to use when it is time to create one of your own classes:

```
class Vehicle(object):
#constructor
def_init_(self, steering, wheels, clutch, breaks, gears):
self._steering = steering
self._wheels = wheels
self._clutch = clutch
self._breaks =breaks
self._gears  = gears
#destructor
def_del_(self):
    print("This is destructor....")
```

```
#member functions or methods

def Display_Vehicle(self):

    print('Steering:' , self._steering)

    print('Wheels:', self._wheels)

    print('Clutch:', self._clutch)

    print('Breaks:', self._breaks)

    print('Gears:', self._gears)

#instantiate a vehicle option

myGenericVehicle = Vehicle('Power Steering', 4, 'Super Clutch', 'Disk Breaks', 5)


myGenericVehicle.Display_Vehicle()
```

Before we move on with this one, we need to take the time to add this into a compiler and see what happens. Just open up the text editor that you are working with and type up the code that we have above. As you write this out, see if you are able to recognize a few of the different topics that we have discussed already in this guidebook! Once you have finished typing this code in, it is time to look at the different parts.

We need to divide this up a bit and take a closer look at how it is all going to work together. Our first goal here is to look at the class definition and how it is going to show up in the code. This definition of the class is important because it is where you can instantiate the object, and then you can add the definition back into the class. The reason for all of this is that you will be able to write it out so that the class is written and is able to hold onto any objects that you place inside.

When you work with the class definition, it is important to pay attention to what you define it as because this part will tell the compiler what it needs to do. If you are looking to get a new definition of the class added into the code, you have a few functions to make this happen. The two that work the best for this include object_attribute and object_method, to make sure that the definition works the best for you.

After we have worked with the class definition, it is time to look at with these classes will include the special attributes. These special attributes are going to be important with this one because they will provide you with a bit of extra security that the code is going to work the way that you want, without errors and other issues along the way.

In the code that we were doing before has some of the special attributes. We used this in order to make sure that the classes and the objects were going to end up in the right spot each time. That is just one example of a special attribute that works with classes. A few of the other options that you can learn about when you want to create your own classes include:

- __bases__: this is considered a tuple that contains any of the superclasses

- __module__: this is where you are going to find the name of the module and it will also hold your classes.

- __name__: this will hold on to the class name.

- __doc__: this is where you are going to find the reference string inside the document for your class.

- __dict__: this is going to be the variable for the dict. Inside the class name.

Now that we have had a chance to look at the special attributes that go with creating a class, it is time to look at another thing that will help us. This part is going to help us to access a few of the members that come in the class that you just created. This needs to be done in order to ensure that the compiler and the text editor are able to recognize the new class that you created and that it will show up in your program as well. To help you see the way that you are able to access the members of any class that has been created, you can use a code like the way below:

```
class Cat(object)
    itsAge = None
    itsWeight = None
    itsName = None
    #set accessor function use to assign values to the fields or member vars
    def setItsAge(self, itsAge):
    self.itsAge = itsAge
```

```python
    def setItsWeight(self, itsWeight):
        self.itsWeight = itsWeight

    def setItsName(self, itsName):
        self.itsName = itsName

    #get accessor function use to return the values from a field
    def getItsAge(self):
        return self.itsAge

    def getItsWeight(self):
        return self.itsWeight

    def getItsName(self):
        return self.itsName


objFrisky = Cat()
objFrisky.setItsAge(5)
objFrisky.setItsWeight(10)
objFrisky.setItsName("Frisky")
print("Cats Name is:", objFrisky.getItsname())
print("Its age is:", objFrisky.getItsAge())
print("Its weight is:", objFrisky.getItsName())
```

Take a moment to type this into your compiler and have it run. You are going to be able to see the results of the code show up on your screen right away. This is going to include things like the name of the cat, as Frisky, along with all of the other things that we had placed in there. You do have the freedom to add in different options and experiment a bit to see what is going to happen as you do that.

You can see that a class is not going to be that difficult to work with. They are the perfect thing to use in order to take care of all the different information that is in your code and to keep it all in order so that it comes up when you want, and in the right order. You are able to create any kind of class as you would, and fill it up with any of the objects that you would like. If you use the syntax above as your guide for making classes, you will be set to get these done in no time.

A look at the objects.

Now that we have had some time to look at the classes that you are able to write out in your code, it is time to look at some of the objects, and how these two topics are going to relate back to one another. To keep this simple, the objects are going to be the part of the code that you will place into the classes that you are going to create.

You can have as many objects as you would like in your code, and you can fit as many of them into each class as you would like. But there are a few rules that you should go with to make sure it all falls in line with what is allowed with the code.

First, when you are creating a class, it can be any kind that you would like. And you can add in any kind of object that you would like. Keep in mind that in one class, you need to make sure, when someone looks at it; it makes sense why all of those objects are in the same class. They do not have to be exactly the same; you could have a class that is all animals, rather than just ones that are elephants. But it needs to make sense why all of the items are in the same class.

Working with objects and classes are going to help you to really see some results with the kind of code that you want to right. The classes are going to hold onto all of the different objects that you are going into the code, and will ensure that you are able to get things to show up at the right time when your code is ready to execute. Experiment a bit with the code by adding it into your compiler to make sure that you are able to create the classes and the objects that you would like to make in your codes.

Chapter 10: The Python Iterators

The Python iterators are a fun thing to add into your code if it is going to work with the kind of program that you will need. The iterators in Python are going to be any kind of object that you add into the code that is going to allow for an iteration over a collection. Now, you will find that these collections do not have to object that is found in the computer memory, and because of this, it is possible to make some objects that are infinite if you choose.

Let us be a bit more precise with the definition that we are using. You can easily say that an iterable is an item that has an "__inter__' method needed in returning an iterator object. IT is also possible that an iterator is an object containing the '__inter__' method and the '__next__' or you can use simply 'next'. When you look at the former, you are going to get an iterator object and then the latter is going to return the subsequent elements of the iteration.

When you work on your code, you want to avoid calling 'next' and __inter__ directly. Python is going to help you call these up automatically if you use a list or 'for' comprehensions. In case you do need to go through and call them up manually, you can use the included in the functions of 'inter' and 'next' in Python and then pass the container or iterator as the restriction.

Yes, this one does seem to be a bit more complicated, but if you are using the Python language to work with some mathematics, you will love working with these iterators. Python is a great language that has libraries and more that can support the mathematics that you would like to use. For example, you can use things like notations, tuples, sets, and lists to help you get mathematical things done in this language.

The biggest thing that you may like when you decide to work with Python if you have a mind that is mathematical is these iterators, as well as the generators that we talked about at an earlier time in this guidebook. Both the iterator and the generator can help to make it easier for the programmer to go through and write out some more complex code. To help us see some of the different things that you are able to do when you introduce the iterator in the Python code that you are writing.

Understanding what iterators are all about

We spent a bit of time above talking about what iterators are, but we are going to dive into this a bit more and see what they are and how you are able to use them in your code. To keep things simple, the iterator is going to be any kind of object that you add into your code that is able to iterate throughout the collection. The collection can be new objects that you create or ones that are found in the memory already.

The tables that you use in the code are going to be defined as objects that are going to call on the method known as __iter__, and this is going to be the method that you want to return back to the object that is your iterator. In this case, it is possible to get this kind of iterator to work with two methods at the same time. The two methods that work with this one include the __iter__ and the __next__ method. With the __next__ method, you will need to use it any time that you want to get the method to return to the object of the iterator. However, with the other one, you are going to ask the compiler to return the element that ends up in the iterator. Because the iterator is going to be its own iterator, it is always going to be able to return the method of __self-_ in the method of the iterator.

Now, at this point, we need to make sure that our code is working well, and to make sure that the things inside the code still make sense when you are coding. To make this happen, programmers will usually choose to not bring out either of the methods directly in their code. Instead, they are going to work with the list comprehension. Python will go through and automatically set this up. However, double-check on this because depending on the code, you may need to do a bit of manual work to get it called up, using a few special functions found in Python.

At this point in the process, we need to actually look at the steps that you are able to take in order to work with the iterators in Python. We are going to make the letter "b" be iterable that we want. If this is our iterable, you would be able to write out either iter(b) or d.__iter__() to get the answer or to make the code work. Either of these is fine and the compiler will read them the same, but the first option is going to be simpler to read and write out.

A note to keep in mind here is that when you decide to work with what is known as the len) function, the iterator is not going to have a defined length that you are able to use here. This is going to be true most of the time when you try to do some iterators in Python. However, the good news is that with the len() function, it isn't very often that you will use it at all. If you do need to bring it out, you can look inside the iterator and see the number of items inside of it, then do the work manually to get it to work.

An example of how these iterators work:

Some tables will contain other objects, which will serve as their iterators, and this means that they are not going to be iterators themselves. For instance, the object 'list" is iterable but not at all an iterator (instead of implementing next, it is going to implement __inter__). As you can see in the example that we are going to have below, iterators for the 'list' objects are going to use 'listiterator' type. You may even observe how the 'list' objects contained a properly establish length, and the listiterato objects do not have that.

```
>>> a = [1, 2]
>>> type(a)
<type 'list'>
```

```
>>>type(iter(a))

<type'listiterator'>

>>>it = itera)

>>>next(it)

1

>>>next(it)

2

>>>next(it)

Traceback (most recent call last):

File "<stdin>", line 1, in <module>

StopIteration

>>>len(a)

2

>>>len(it)

Traceback(most recent call last):

File "<stdin>", line 1, in <module>

TypeError: object of type 'listiterator' has no len()
```

When this iterator is all done and typed into the compiler well, the interpreter is going to expect it to come out with an exception raised. This particular exception is going to be called "StopIteration". However, when you are working with an iterator, it is technically going to keep going over a set that is endless. These are going to be able to dictate that the user should make sure they are not using the program in any manner that creates a loop that keeps going on and on. You may find that manually fixing this can be the best bet to ensure that any loops you add into the code won't get stuck and freeze up your program.

Chapter 11: Starting with the Python Generators

The next idea that we are going to take a look at here is the idea of the generators. The generators that show up in Python are going to be functions that will ensure you can create a sequence of results. The reason that we look at them is that the generators are able to maintain a state that is known as their local state, ensuring that the function is able to resume right back where they left off if they had to be called up more than one time.

This may sound a bit confusing, but as you work through a few of the different codes that we study in this guidebook, you will find that it starts to make a bit more sense as time goes on. You can think of the generator as a really strong and powerful iterator. The function state will be maintained as we talked about before when you bring in the keyword of "yield". In Python, this is similar to hitting the return button, but we do need to explore a few of the differences, as well as more information on how these generators can come into play in your codes.

How to make these generators work?

There are many things that the generator is going to be able to do when it comes to making your code behave, and ensuring that you do not have to restart the code all over again when you call up a function more than once. However, you will find that one of the best ways to make sure that we have a full understanding of how these generators work is to look at an example, such as the one we will provide to you below:

```
# generator_example_1.py


Def numberGenerator(n):
    Number = 0
    While number < n:
    Yield number
    Number + = 1


myGenerator = numberGenerator(3)


print(next(myGenerator))
print(next(myGeneartor))
print(next(myGenerator))
```

The code that we have above is going to define a generator for you with the name 'numberGenerator' that gest the value 'n' as the argument before you go through and define it using a while loop to help with a limit value. In addition, it is going through and helping you define a variable that has the name of 'number' and then it assigns a zero value with this.

When you call in your instantiated generator using the 'myGenerator with the method 'next()' in it, it is going to go through and run your generator through the code until the initial 'yield' statement. For this example, it is going to return 1. Even when you get a value returned to you, your function is going to tend to keep the variable 'number' value for when you call up your function next, and then it grows in value by one. What this means is that it is able to start up again right where it left off at the next call of the function.

Now, it is possible for you to call up a generator once more after this. If this is what you decide to do, you just need to keep following what we have already placed into the code, but then this is going raise up an exception. This exception is going to say "StopIteration" simply because it has finished up and reverted from the internal while loop at this point.

This may make it seem frustrating and like you are not able to do what you want with the code, but this can be useful when it comes to adding this into your code. The use of the generator in this manner is going to help you create a few of the iterables that you need as you go through this.

Let us say that you have gone through on your code and you were able to use the list() to wrap 'myGenerator'. When this happens, you are going to get an array of numbers back as the answer, rather than the generator object that you would like. In some instances though, this is going to make life a bit easier for you to do and work with.

Looking at how between and yield are going to be different.

It is time to look at another point that shows up when you work with the generators. There will be times in this process where the "return" keyword is going to be the one to use. This is going to happen when you want to get a return of a value from the given function. When you do this, the function is going to get lost out of the local state and this can make it difficult to run the code that you want.

What all of this is going to mean is that when you go through and need to call up the function once more, or as frequently as you would like, the code will not have a reference point to call up. You will have to go and start all the way from the top in the first statement. You can easily see why this is going to cause some problems if you are not careful.

Then there is the option of using the keyword of 'yield'. This one is going to be brought out when you want to make sure that you want to keep the state of the function, without having to start all the way over. You can choose when you want to go back with the function or when it is time to start over, giving you a bit more control, this is why using the generators, and working with the yield keyword can be really useful for many of your codes.

The returned generator

The generator can use the statement for 'return' but only when there is no return value. The generator will then go on as in any other function return when it reaches this statement. The return tells the program that you are done and you want it to go back to the rest of the code. Let us take a look at how you can change up the code to use these generators simply by adding in an if-else clause so that you can discriminate against any numbers that are above 20. The code you would use for this includes:

```
# geneator_example_2.py

def numberGeneator(n):
        if n < 20:
        number = 0
        while number < n:
        yield number
        number +=1
else:
        return
print(list(numberGeneator(30)))
```

This particular example is going to show that the genitor will be an empty array. This is because we have set it so that it will not yield any values that are above 20. Since 30 is above 20, you will not get any results with this one. In this particular case, the return statement is going to work in the same way as a break statement. However, if you go through this code and you get a value that is below 20, you would then see that show up in the code.

More to learn about the generators

The thing to remember with these generators is that they are a type of iterator, an iterator that the code has been able to define with a notation of the function so that the function is easier to use in the code. When you decide to work with the generator, you are basically working with a type of function that is able to give you a yield expression. These will not be able to give you the return value that you may expect though.

Instead of doing this, when it is time to use the generators, they are going to just provide you with the results. The process that you should remember with this is that you need the generator to be an automated process in Python otherwise; it is going to become too complicated and may not work.

Now, you will find that there are a few options that you can use when it comes to calling up any generator that is available for you to use. If you call up the generator using the ___next___ keyword, the yield you are going to get will show up in the next iteration value in the line. This is not the only option that is available though and you can work with the ___iter___, which is one that will make sure your program is implemented automatically while telling the program that it needs to take the generator and move it back to the place where the iterator is needed.

As you go through and work on your code and you find that you need to add in a generator at some point, there are going to be a few options to choose from to make it easier. Some of the different options that you are able to work with include:

1. Generator expressions: These expressions are helpful to work with because they will help the programmer to define the generator with the help of simple notation. This is easier, and you can easily do it any time that you create a list using the Python language. You can use the two methods that we have above, the __next__ and __iter__ to make it happen because these provide you with the results for any type of generator that you want to create.

2. Recursive generators: It is possible for your chosen generator to be recursive, just like what you are able to find with some functions. The idea that you get with this one is that you would need to swap out all of the elements that you have on your list with the one that ends up on top. This helps all of the elements to move up and the list will slowly start to disappear as you do this.

When are some times that I need generators?

We have spent some time in this chapter talking about generators and how you are able to use them, but now it is time to take a look at when you might actually use the generators to help you get things done. We did a few examples of these generators through this guidebook, and you can see that they are a more advanced tool that can be used to write out codes.

As a beginner, it is possible that you will not use these generators all that much. It may seem like they are too difficult, but knowing how to make them work can ensure that there is some kind of efficiency when it comes to the program you are trying to write. Some of the scenarios where you may find that using these generators is going to be helpful can include the following:

1. Any time that you as the programmer end up with a ton of data that you think needs to be processed. The generators help with this because they are going to be able to offer a calculation based on the demand. This is a good option to use when you want to finish a project like stream processing.

2. You may find that working with a stacked generator can mean that you are working with the process of piping. This is the same way that you would be able to use the Unix pipes. To make this easier, you are able to use the generator in order to pipeline a series of operations to make it easier to work with.

As you can see, the generators are going to be a wonderful addition to the process that allows you to have a lot of freedom in what you are doing, can make sure that you are able to get back to the part of the code where you want to be, and can generally make your life easier rather than having to plan for the code restarting all of the time. It may be a bit more than what some beginners want to add into their codes, but it can make a world of difference in how efficient and easy your code is to work with.

Chapter 12: Is It Important to Work with Assert Handling with Python?

Now it is time to take our work in a different direction. We are going to take some time to learn about assertions in Python. These are somewhat similar to what we have looked at with a few other topics, but it is still important to discover the differences that come with it. You will see that assertions are most likely to come up when exception handling is discussed, and often you will need to handle both of these topics at the same time. This is why we are going to take some time to look at assert handling now.

When we talk about assertion within the Python language, we are looking at something that is kind of like a check for how well the code is going to work. Either you can choose to have it off or one when you are completed with the testing portion of your program. The effortless way to think about an affirmation is that it is like a raise if statement or a raise if not statement. If you are testing the exception, and you end up with the latter one showing up, you will notice that the exception has been raised in the program.

You will need to use the assert statement in order to help make sure the assertion is carried out. This is going to be a newer keyword, and you may not be able to find it in some of the older versions of Python if you choose to go with these. Many programs find that it is easiest to place the assertions at the way beginning of the function because this helps you to double-check the function and see if it has an input that is valid. They may also put it after calling up a function to check if the output is valid to use as well.

Looking more at the assert statement

When you are working to add in one of these assert statements in any code, the program in Python is set up to evaluate the expression that follows this statement. The hope here is that the answer is true and you will get to move on with the code. However, there are going to be times when the statement is going to evaluate the part of the code and will find that the expression is false. This is when the exception is known as AssertionError. The syntax that we will see when using this one includes:

assert Expression [, Arguments]

If you use this and the assertion fails, Python is going to use ArgumentExression as your argument for this error. These types of exceptions can be caught, and you can handle them similarly, to what we did earlier with exception handling. You can employ the try-except statement to help you deal with it properly.

There will be times when the Python code will not be able to handle the exception that is raised with that statement. If the program cannot handle it, then it is going to terminate your program and will produce a traceback. However, for the most part, this assertion is going to help you handle any issues that come up and it is mostly there to help you catch anything that can go wrong in the program.

Learning how to do assertion handling is going to be important to any type of code that you choose to write. It is going to make sure that if there is an issue inside of your code, you are able to catch it and handle it before you send that program out to the world. It gives you the option of checking out if the statement you wrote is true or not whether the program is able to handle this on its own, or if it is time to fix a few errors or bugs that, you may have made inside of that program.

No matter why you decide to use it, or whether or not it finds the bug or mistake that is there (sometimes there are no bugs or mistakes), assertions can be helpful. This is even truer if you are working with any kind of exception in the code. It is effective, it is safe, and it only adds a few more lines of code overall to make sure that the whole program is going to work in the proper manner.

Why should I take the time to test my code?

One of the things that you are able to do with the assert statement is to test your code in certain areas and make sure that it works. It gets the program to go through and perform a test so that you catch bugs or potential problems before you release the program. Getting used to not only writing the code but also writing out some testing code and running it with the regular code can make sure that your program always works the way that you want.

When you are able to use this process in the proper manner, you will find that the assert statements are going to be a good way to help you define the intent of any code you write and to make sure that it works the way that you want. However, if you are still uncertain about why you need to work with assert statements, there are many great rules to follow, including:

1. When you pick out the unit that you are going to use in the testing, you want to make sure this unit is able to keep its focus on the functionality that the code has. Its job is to prove that this part of the code works properly and is correct.

2. You will do many different units and each of them needs to work on their own, rather than together. Each of the tests that you write need to be able to run on their own, along with the test suite, even if they are called up in a different order.

   a. The idea with this kind of rule is that your test should be loaded up with a new data set and it needs to clean up as well when it is done. The two methods that you can add to your assert statement to make this happen to include the setup() method and the teardown() method.

3. When you are designing a new test, you need to make sure that the code you write is able to run fairly quickly. If it does not, then this is really going

to slow down what you are able to do with the code. Complex data and more can slow this process down, but you want to make sure that the test is able to go through and do the work that you want, without slowing the program down that you are working on.

4. There are many different tools that you are able to work within your programming, and it is important to learn how to use them as well as possible. You also want to make sure that the tests are set up as often as possible. Do so automatically and at any time that you stop to save the code to make sure that your code works well.

5. Before you start with a new session of the coding, you need to go through and do a full test suite run. And when you are all done, go through and run that test again. This helps you to add in some more confidence about the code you are writing and ensures that nothing is broken before or after a code writing session.

6. If you are working on a development session and then have to leave right in the middle, you can write in a broken unit test about what you are planning on working on next. Then, when you come back to the work, you will still have a point there where you can get right back on track.

7. When you are doing code and trying to debug it, you should work on a new test that is responsible for finding the bug. This is not always something that is possible, but the bug-catching tests are going to be very valuable when you do your project.

8. When you are testing out a function, make sure that you use descriptive and long names. The style guide for this point is often going to be a bit

different than what you would do when running a code; for those, you want names that are somewhat short. The reason that your testing functions need to be longer is that you want them to display on the screen when the test fails. When you have them as descriptive as possible, it is easier to tell what is going on in the code.

9. Anytime that you are doing something with your code, and it does not function the way that you want it to, or you need to make sure that something gets changed, and you have already been able to do the testing, this means that the testing suite can be used here to fix this problem. The testing code needs to be read as much if not more than the code you decide to run.

   a. Now, it is not necessarily a bad thing to rely on the testing code to help you out. However, taking the right precautions and making sure that you test the code to check for the accuracy of the code.

10. Another way that you are able to use the testing code to make sure that everything lines up well is to introduce another developer to the mix. They are going to look through the testing code and double-check things for you. Since they are not close to the code at all and have not been working with it, they will be a fresh pair of eyes to ensure that you will be able to catch all of the bugs and other issues that come with it.

It is tempting to avoid some of the testings that need to be done with your code. But doing this kind of testing is going to make sure that any code you decide to work with is free of errors or any bugs so that it works well. You should make sure that you use the assert statement rules that we have above, and you will be able to always test your code and make sure that it works the way that you would like from the beginning.

Chapter 13: Using Closures Properly in Python to Get Your Codes Done

The next item that we need to take a look at when we try to develop a code in Python is the idea of closures. However, before we jump into this too far, we need to be able to understand a few of the other parts that come with the Python language. Nested functions and non-local variables are going to be needed with this kind of code, and they will help us to really work on the closures and get them to work well for us. With this in mind, we are going to first take a look at the nested functions.

First, what is a nested function? Any time that you have one function that you want to use and you need to define it inside of a different kind of function, the first one is going to be established as the nested function. These nested functions are going to be interesting to work with because of how you create them and their ability to approach variables of the enclosing scope. In Python, though the non-local variables can be accessed only when you are in the current scope, and any scope that is not there will not be able to find them. Let us examine at an example of how this is going to work:

 # Python program to illustrate

 # nested functions

def outerFunction(text):

```
text = text


def innerFunction():

    print(text)


innerFunction()


if __name__ == '__main__':

    outerFunction('Hey!')
```

As you can see here, the innerFunction() part of the code is something that your outerFunction can access, and you can use it as much as you want as long as you are in that function. However, if you leave this, or go to another part of the code, you will not be able to access that innerFunction() part. In this case, the innerFunction() is going to be the nested function, which will use text as its non-local variable.

What are these closures?

Now that we have had a chance to look at the nested function and see what they are, as well as a look at the non-local variables, it is time to bring in the idea of the closure. The closure is going to be an object of the function that is responsible for remembering the values that you add into the enclosing scope. This is going to happen, even when the objects will not show up in the memory of the computer that you use.

The closure is going to be like a new record that is responsible for storing the function, along with the environment and we can look at it as a mapping that associates all of the variables in the function that ends up being free. As we go through with this, remember that the variables that are found here are going to be used locally, but they will be defined in their enclosing scope. You are able to do this thanks to the value or the reference that you bound to the namespace of the closure the first time that you created it.

If you have worked with the plain function in the past, you will find that the closure is going to be a bit different. The closure comes in and makes it so that the function is able to access the variables that you end up capturing, and it does this by going through the closures copies of the references or its copies of the values. This is possible and can happen even when the function is called up outside of its own scope. Let us take a glimpse at how this is going to work and some of the things that you can do to get the best results.

```python
# Python program to illustrate
# closures
def outerFunction(text):
    text = text
```

```
def innerFunction():

    print(text)


return innerFunction # Note we are returning function WITHOUT
parenthesis


if __name__ == '__main__':
  myFunction = outerFunction('Hey!')
  myFunction()
```

Take a moment to type this code into your compiler and see what happens. What you should be able to observe from this code is that the closure is there to help you call the function up, even when you are not in the right scope. The function is known as innerFunction(has its scope present only in your outerFunction. However, when you use one of these closures, as we did before, you are able to extend the scope so you can call it up anywhere that you would like.

The code above did the same thing that we did originally; make it so that the nested function is called up only inside its original function. However, if you want to be able to call up the function at any point, even when you are outside its scope, you would need to use a code like this one:

```
# Python program to illustrate
# closures
```

```python
import logging
logging.basicConfig(filename='example.log', level=logging.INFO)


def logger(func):
    def log_func(*args):
        logging.info(
            'Running "{}" with arguments {}'.format(func.__name__, args))
        print(func(*args))
    # Necessary for closure to work (returning WITHOUT parenthesis)
    return log_func


def add(x, y):
    return x+y


def sub(x, y):
    return x-y


add_logger = logger(add)
sub_logger = logger(sub)


add_logger(3, 3)
add_logger(4, 5)
```

sub_logger(10, 5)

sub_logger(20, 10)

If you are curious about the differences that show up in the two codes that we have just done, you can take a look at how they react when brought up in your compiler. When you do this, you are going to see that the output between the two will be a bit different, which is going to help you see how these closures work so well in your code. Learning how these works in a similar manner and how they are different will make it much easier for you to use them no matter what scope you have in mind.

The biggest decision that you need to make when you are using this is whether you would like the chance to reach the nested function only when it is inside of the original function you placed it, would you like the option, or will need the option, to reach it no matter where you are in the code. For the first option, you just need to work with the first code earlier in this chapter, and for the second one, you need to make sure that the closure is there to help you, like what we just did above.

When is a closure necessary?

As we have been able to talk about a bit in this guidebook, there are a few different situations where you would need to add some kind of closure into the code that you are writing. However, we will go over them very quick to make sure you are familiar when they are going to come into play, and when they may be necessary for your success.

The first reason that you would want to use closures is that they can be a great callback function when needed. This means that you are able to use the closure to provide you with a manner of hiding any data that you want. In your code, this can reduce the number of global variables that are available, but this is a good thing. Reducing the number of those variables is going to reduce the bugs that show up and can make it cleaner and nicer.

Another benefit of working with these closures in your code is that they make the functions work better. If you have two or more functions that need to work at the same time or really close together, the closures are an efficient and good manner to deal with all of them. However, if the number of functions gets too high, and you need to work with quite a few of them in your code, you will need to result in the classes instead.

The best way to tell if you need to work with a closure or not is the end result that you want to see when it is all done. Some programmers find that there really isn't a need for them to access the nested function other than in the current scope, so they would not need to work with the closures and adding one in is more time and work than necessary.

Then there are going to be times when the closures are necessary to make the code work the way that you would like. If you need the function to not only show up in your local scope if this is something that your code needs to see happen, then working with the closure is going to make this happen in a more successful manner.

Chapter 14: Creating Your Own Inheritances

Inheritances are another neat idea that you are able to create when working on your own Python code. This one is going to take some writing out and may seem a bit longer and more work compared to the others, but once it gets put into the code, you will find that it actually helps the code to flow easier, and will ensure that your code works the way that you would like.

When you bring out an inheritance that you want to work with, you will find that they are going to make sure that you can write out a ton of code that is complex, without having to go through and write out every line. This cleans up the code, helps it to look nicer, and can save you some time and effort all at the same time.

To help us get started when it comes to how these inheritances are going to work, we need to know what this is all about. The inheritance is going to be when you write out some code, and then you turn that into the parent code. You can then copy it down and make some changes, without changing up the original code, and make a brand new child code. The child code is completely adjustable along the way so that you are able to add and take things away as you need, and the parent code from before will still work the same.

You can go on down the line with this as well. You can just have one parent code and one child code, or you can make your own family tree of inheritances with this idea. Moreover, each child code is able to be adjusted and changed so that you end up with exactly what you need, without having any effect on the code that is being used as the parent.

While an inheritance may sound complex, it is a simple code to learn. You can add or take away as much as you want to get this code to work the way that you want. A good example of how an inheritance looks like inside of your code includes the following:

```
#Example of inheritance
#base class
class Student(object):
        def__init__(self, name, rollno):
        self.name = name
        self.rollno = rollno
#Graduate class inherits or derived from Student class
class GraduateStudent(Student):
        def__init__(self, name, rollno, graduate):
        Student__init__(self, name, rollno)
        self.graduate = graduate

def DisplayGraduateStudent(self):
        print"Student Name:", self.name)
        print("Student Rollno:", self.rollno)
```

```
        print("Study Group:", self.graduate)


#Post Graduate class inherits from Student class
class PostGraduate(Student):
        def __init__(self, name, rollno, postgrad):
        Student __init__(self, name, rollno)
        self.postgrad = postgrad


        def DisplayPostGraduateStudent(self):
        print("Student Name:", self.name)
        print("Student Rollno:", self.rollno)
        print("Study Group:", self.postgrad)


#instantiate from Graduate and PostGraduate classes
        objGradStudent = GraduateStudent("Mainu", 1, "MS-Mathematics")
        objPostGradStudent = PostGraduate("Shainu", 2, "MS-CS")
        objPostGradStudent.DisplayPostGraduateStudent()
```

When you type this into your interpreter, you are going to get the results:

```
('Student Name:', 'Mainu')
('Student Rollno:', 1)
('Student Group:', 'MSC-Mathematics')
('Student Name:', 'Shainu')
```

('Student Rollno:', 2)

('Student Group:', 'MSC-CS')

As you are working on this code, you will love that the inheritance will provide you with some freedom. If you already have a code written out that you like many features of, and you want to reuse them, you can do this with the help of inheritances, without having to go through and write the code a bunch of times. In addition, you can take the new child or derived code and rewrite it and add in the features that you want, and you will love the different processes that are available with this option in Python.

Another thing to remember with the inheritances is that you can really go through and add in as many derived classes as you would like. The only rules here are that you keep going down the line in order with one another, and you use a syntax similar to the one above. If you can do this, your derived classes can fill up lots of lines of code if that is what works the best for the program you are writing at the time.

The ability to write out a ton of derived classes, if you need to, and to have as many of these as you would like is going to make things easier. And each of the new derived classes that you are working on gets the benefits of taking on features that you want from the base code above, or you can drop some if that makes the program work a bit better.

Can I override one of my base classes?

The next thing that we need to take a look at and discuss when we are creating our own inheritance is how we are able to override one of the base classes that we want to use. There may be some times when you will start to create a derived class, and then you want to change up some things by overriding the base class. Any time that you want to go through and change up some of the features in the base class to create your new derived class, you are going to want to do an override to make this happen.

It is actually a lot easier to work with than it sounds in the beginning, but it basically allows you to take a base class and create an inheritance into a derived class. And then the derived class can override things in order to become brand new and work the way that you want in the code. This ensures that with any new class you make based on the base class, you will get to keep what you want, and then get rid of the things that are in the way or are not working how you want.

The process of overloading

In addition to being able to override some of the objects that are found in the base class when doing inheritances, you are able to work with overloading. When it is time to bring in overloading, this means that you are trying to take one of the identifiers in the code and use it to define at least two methods overall and get that to work in the code.

For the most part, when you do your own override, you will just have two methods, but there may be some situations where you need to work with more than two. These two methods need to be placed in the same class, but the parameters are going to be different so that they can be running in different processes. This overloading process is going to work the best when you have these two methods doing work that follows different parameters so that they can run at the same time, but will not interfere with each other.

As a beginner, there are not that many instances where you will need to use the process of overloading. However, as you start to write some more codes and add into the complexity, this may be something that sneaks in more based on the kind of code and program that you are trying to create.

Some more things to know when it comes to inheritances

We need to take a moment to discuss a few more things about these inheritances and how you are able to work with them in the Python code. The first thing to explore here is how you are able to work with multiple inheritances at once. When you decide to do one of these inheritances, you will find that as you go down the levels, each one is going to share a few similarities with the others, but it is still possible to get to a new level and make the changes that are needed.

The multiple inheritances may take a few more steps to get the thing done, but you will find that they are going to be done in the same manner that we did the single one, and you can just add to that example when you want to create one. You just need to keep moving down the line until you are done with all of the inheritances that you want to create.

When you are working on a program where you will need to code multiple inheritances, you will need to take one class, which is again going to be that base class, and you will give it at least two child classes to get started. This is important as you work with growing your code because it is going to help you get the inheritances to go down as far as you would like.

Multiple inheritances can be as simple or as complicated as you would like to make them. When you work on them, you will be able to create a brand new class, which we will call Class C, and you got the information to create this new class from the previous one, or Class B. Then you can go back and find that Class B was the one that you created from information out of Class A. Each of these layers is going to contain some features that you like from the class ahead of it, and you can go as far into it as you would like. Depending on the code that you decide to write, you could have ten or more of these classes, each level having features from the previous one to keep it going.

While you are working to create multiple inheritances, remember that you can go down the levels, as many times as you would like, but you are not allowed to do what is known as a circular inheritance? You can have as many parent classes that turn into derived classes, but you cannot make it go in a circle, and then connect things from the top with this method, or you are going to end up with an error in the code along the way.

As you can see, there are many different things that you are able to do with these inheritances. It can help you to save some time using the features that you like from the parent class, and it will ensure that you are able to clean up the code. Yes, the code example that we did above may look long, but it was there to give us an idea of how to work with the classes, both the base and the derived. In addition, if you had to write these out without using the idea of inheritances, imagine how many lines of code you have to write.

As you start to write more and more codes and make your own programs with the help of the Python language, you will find that there are going to be some inheritance types that you are able to use, because these are pretty popular. There are many times when you can just use the base code and use it to make a new piece of code, without having to waste a lot of time in order to rewrite the code again all of the time. It is as simple as this and can make your code really work well, without as much work.

Chapter 15: Bringing in the Descriptors

Another topic that we need to take a look at when working in the Python language is the idea of the descriptors. These descriptors come up a lot in your codes so it is a good idea for us to learn how to make these work. You can write some codes without these, but many times adding the descriptors to your code can help you to get a nice edge over the competition when you are working on any code that you would like. With this in mind though, they are sometimes a bit difficult to understand. This is why we are going to focus on a practical example to show us exactly how and when we would try to use these descriptors in one of our Python codes.

Imagine that you are trying to work with a new program that needs to be able to do some strict type checking of all the object attributes that show up. Since we see that Python is known as a dynamic language, there is not really support available for type checking, but this does not mean that you are stuck here. You are able to create your own program with the help of the descriptors that will help you to get this done.

Of course, it would be easier to work with some of the conventional methods and have the program do this for you. However, this is not available when you are working with Python, and any of the options that this language provides to you will not work in the right manner. Take a moment to look over the example that we have below and see if you are able to spot where the problem may be with this part of the code:

```
Def __init__(self, name, age):
        If isinstance(str, name):
        Self.name = name
        Else:
                Raise Type Error("Must be a string")
        If isinstance(int, age):
        Self.age = age
        Else:
        Raise TypeError("Must be an int")
```

This method is one way that you are able to enforce the type checking if you want to use it, but this can become a mess if you start to add in some more arguments. There is a little easier way to get this done. Using the type_check(type, val) function, you can do the same thing as well. This part would need to be called before your assignment with the __init__ method, but then how would we be able to implement this particular checking when we want to place the attribute value set somewhere else? Some programmers will go to the Java method of setters and getters, but this does not work all that well when you work inside Python.

At some point, you may be interested in creating some kind of program that can add in an attribute to just one of the routines, rather than all of them, and then you want to turn the file around and ensure it is a read-only file. There are a few different methods that you are able to choose with this one, but they are all a bit cumbersome to use.

This is where the idea of the descriptors can come into play and will be useful. They are designed to help you work on any kind of program you are customizing so that you can have a chance to access the attributes of that object. You can use this for many options, including for log access, and even to reuse parts of the code, as you need them in your program.

This brings us to the point of how the descriptors can be used to help with all of this. The solution to some of the issues where descriptors are going to be super useful is to just add it in. the descriptor in Python is an object that is going to be the representation of the attribute value. What this means is that if the account object named the attribute, then the descriptor is going to be an object that is going to hold onto the value of the attribute. A descriptor is going to have the ability to be any of the objects that show up in your code, as long as you implement them with the methods of __get__, __set__, and __delete__.

If you are using an object that is in need of the special method known as __get__, then it is going to be known as a non-data descriptor. What this means to the code is that these objects, in particular, are going to only be read after they are through with the initialization. But one that is going to work with both the ___get___ and the ___set___ method will be called the data descriptors, which means that you get to take the attribute and write on it.

This may be a bit hard to understand when you get started, but we have some code to help you learn how these descriptors work and what they are able to do. We are going to take a look at some of the solutions that came with the issues we talked about earlier. This will help you to type checking implementation easier to work with. The code that you would use to help a decorator implement type checking would be like the syntax below:

```
Class TypedProperty(object):
        Def__init__(self, name, type, default=None):
            Self.name = "_" + name
        Self.type = type
        Self.default = default if default else type()
Def__get__(self, instance, cls):
        Return getarttr(instance, self.name, self.default)
Def__set__(self, instance, value):
        If not isinstance(value, selt.type):
        Raise Type Error("Must b a %*% self.type)
        Sestattr(instance, self.name, value)
Def__delete__(self, instance):
        Raise AttributeError("Cannot delete this attribute")
```

```
Class Foo(object(

        Name = TypedProperty("name', str)

        Num = TypedProperty("um", int, 42)


>>acct = Foo()

>>>acct.name = "obit"

>>>acct.num = 1234

>>>print acct.num

1234

>>>print acct.name

Obi

# attempting to assign a string to a number does not work

>>>acct.num = '1234'

Type Error: This must be a <type "int">
```

Once you have a chance to add all of the code above into your compiler, it is time to break it up a little bit. This may seem like a lot in the beginning, but we will look it over and go through it by steps to figure out what is happening, and how the descriptor was able to come in and help make the code work the way that you want.

What we ended up doing in the code above was to implement the descriptor that we called TypedProperty. This is going to be the class that is used to enforce the type checking on any of the attributes that you want within this code, as long as you make sure that all of the processes happen inside the represented class. Be aware of this that the descriptor is going to happen outside of the instance level, and only inside of your class level.

Now we need to explore a bit about the class instance. When we work to get to the attribute and access it, you will need to use the method known as __get__() for the descriptor. The first argument at this point to bring up for the method will be that the attribute is represented by the descriptor references. Then we move on to the __set__ method so that the descriptor is able to call that up the moment the attribute is given an assignment.

We are getting ahead of ourselves with this, and to help us get a better understanding of what all is happening with the code, and to understand why the descriptor is used to represent the attribute, you have to understand how Python is able to carry out the process that resolves your attributes. Any time that you are working with a type of object in this scenario, we are going to use object.__getattribute__() to help us get the compiler to provide us with the resolutions. This needs to be added into the code to ensure this happens.

From this point, we are going to move on to look at how the resolution comes and how we can use it as part of the precedence chain. This chain is used to ensure we are looking for the right attributes inside of the code, rather than just looking around and hoping we find something, but maybe getting it wrong. The chain is important here because at this point in the code, it is going to provide you with the descriptors that tie back to the data provided, which will show up (in this example) in the dict class, and these will have a priority over the instance variables.

While we are on the variables and which ones are getting priority and so on, keep in mind that the variables are going to have some precedence when it comes to any of the non-data descriptors, and you will find them assigned over the getattr(), which is actually going to be the last thing that the code puts out, because it has the lowest priority out of the group.

Working with descriptors can make a big difference in the kind of code that you are trying to write. It may be possible to write some code that is a bit more straightforward and easier to work with without this. However, as your coding starts to advance and you work with it more and add in some more complexity to it, you will find that there are many times when a descriptor, like the one in this chapter, will be able to come into play and help you to get your code up and running.

Chapter 16: What If Something Goes Wrong with My Coding? How to Fix Common Coding Problems for Beginners

In this guidebook, we have spent a lot of time exploring all of the different topics that come with writing your own codes in Python. We looked at why this is such a popular type of coding language to work with, why you may want to work with this coding language over some of the others, and even some of the steps that you need to take to make sure this coding language is going to work well on your system, no matter which one you go with.

Once some of the basics were out of the way, we explored all of the different parts that can show up in the code. We looked at the basics of coding, how to work with inheritances, generators, loops, conditional statements, exception handling and more. All of these are excellent to learn how to do if you want to start writing some of your own programs in Python.

With that said and done, it is time to move on to troubleshooting your program if something is not working the way that you would like. In an ideal world, you will be able to work on the code and nothing will ever go wrong. However, there are times when your code will not act the way that you want it to. Moreover, as a beginner, this can be really frustrating.

Often the fix for why your program is not working or why you are getting some kind of error message or something else showing up is pretty simple. And it is unlikely that you will want to call someone over to fix simple errors, but you do not want to be stuck either. Even as a beginner though, you are able to learn some of the basic troubleshooting work that will ensure that you can take care of most of the problems that appear in your program, so you can get back to work and create some awesome code. Let us take a glimpse at some of the best troubleshooting tricks and tips that you can follow if your code is not working the way that you want it to work.

Even after small changes, run the code again

The more times that you are able to run your code and check for mistakes, the better you will be. This may seem a bit tedious, but isn't it much better to find an error message after four lines of code, rather than finding it after 1,000 lines of code? Which one would you rather go back and double-check to make sure that nothing is wrong?

You do not want to get into the habit of sitting down with a blank Python file and then spend a few hours coding, without actually trying out any of the code that you are writing. You will just make all of the work that you are doing so much harder for yourself, and when there are a ton of errors that start to show up on your screen, it is confusing to know where to start. It can take forever to go through all of this and fix the issue that is going wrong, and you will probably be ready to give up long before you get anywhere near done.

Instead of putting yourself through that entire headache, consider every few minutes going through and running an update, as well as testing the code out to see how well it works. This way, when one of the messages about an error shows up in the code, you are able to easily pinpoint where the issue is going to be in the code, rather than having to check a ton of it. There is no such thing as testing the code too often, so go crazy with this because it really does make your life easier overall.

Always remember that the more lines of code you decide to write out before doing another test, the more potential errors can come in, and the more time it takes you to go through all of the code and figure it out. Doing the testing more often will make it easier for you to catch the errors and eliminate them quickly. Plus, you will find that doing all of these tests will ensure that you get even more feedback and can learn even more about the coding that you are doing.

Print as many things as you can

As you take a look through your code, you need to be able to look at each line and know ahead of time what values are associated back to each variable. This should be something that is easy for you to do if you wrote out your code in the proper manner. If you look through the code, and you see a value that does not go to a variable or a variable that does not have a value, it is time to stop what you are doing and print out that part of the code. Then, when it is time for you to go through and run the program, you will look back over at the console and see how the values will change, or if these end up turning into a null value in a way that you were not expecting to happen.

There are many times where you will need to print out many different things. You may find that at times you will need to try to print a fixed string before you print out a variable. This will ensure that none of your print statements will end up running together, and then you will have a better idea of where these are going to be printed from.

This can be as simple as complicated as you would like to make it, but basically, any time that you want to check the code, or you want to just make sure that things are working right, and even when things don't look right to you, then it is time to do a print. You can print out something like "print got here" and see whether the code is working well or if there is some kind of mistake in the code that you need to fix.

Actually read through some of the error messages

You will quickly find that many of your error messages are accurate and will actually be pretty descriptive for you. The language runtime tried to execute the program, but it ran into a problem. This would mean that you skipped a step, you had a typo, or something else is missing from your code.

There may be times when you do not understand the message that comes up with an error, but it does try to tell you what went wrong with the code. At a minimum, there will be information on a line number the error is on and you can head to that part of the code and look for where the bug might be located.

It is tempting to see an error message that shows up on the code that you are working on, and not even read it. However, there is a lot of information that you are able to find in the error message, and at least having that information is going to help someone else who comes in and tries to make this easier on you. Taking just a few seconds to read through the error message to see what information you are able to glean from it can make your life easier.

See if a Google search on the error can help

Going back to the idea of the error messages from before, remember that you may not know what all of these error messages are about along the way. It is possible that you see that error message and just sees a block of random letters and numbers that are supposed to go together, and you are not sure what it all means. This is hard to figure out, but there are a few options that are available for you to try out to solve the problem.

Instead of staring at the message in confusion with no idea of what to do next, you can copy and then paste the last line of the stacktract into Google or another search engine and see what comes out. It is very possible that someone else has done some code and received that same error message along the way as well. In addition, they will have asked that question or posted the results of it online somewhere. You can use these answers to help you figure out the next steps to take and how to fix the error.

Depending on the error message that you get, and whether it is pretty specific or generic, you may not be capable to employ this method. It is easier if you can discover it online and get some answers that way. However, there are some situations where this just is not going to happen. This is when you need to just start reading through the code and figure out what the error message is all about and how to fix the problem.

Guess and check

This method may take a bit longer for you to get done, but it could help you out if some of the other methods we talk about just do not seem to be doing the trick. If you try a few of the other methods that we talk about in this chapter, and you still are not able to fix the mistake that is showing up, it is time to do a bit of guessing and checking to see what happens and whether or not this clears up the error that you are getting. Remember that we already talked about the importance of running your code as often as you can, at least after every little section, and this will give you quick feedback to work on.

If you keep up with this, you should have a good idea which part of the code is causing the error. If the error was not there before but shows up after you do a few lines of code, you know that the error is in that new piece of code, and it limits down how much searching that you have to do. You can guess that area and check to see what errors you made.

Now, you do need to be careful with what you are doing here. There can be the possibility in some cases that the fix you try to make will bring in a completely new error to the mixture, and sometimes it is hard to tell whether you are making things more difficult, or if you are actually getting closer to the solution that you want to work with. Try to just make little fixes and see if that helps, rather than doing too much at once and making the situation worse.

Trying out a few options and choices here is going to be important because it will help you to get to the solution faster, while making sure that you really learn about the Python code, without having to ask someone else for help. You will be surprised at how much you are able to learn about coding when you have to troubleshoot your own errors, and you will get better at the coding in the long term by doing this.

Comment out on the code and see if that helps

Every type of coding language that you will work on is going to have the comment, which is basically a way that you can leave a note in your code, without the compiler going through and trying to execute these notes as part of the program. This is advantageous to you because you can choose to comment out of a code that you do not want to run right now, but which you do not want to lose track of. You just need to put the # in front of that line that you want to comment out of.

If your script is long, you can comment on some parts of the code that are not related to the changes that you want to work on. This can sometimes make it run faster and it can make it easier to search through the rest of the code to help find that mistake. You need to be careful when doing this though because it will not help you to comment out of parts that set the variables that the program needs to use later on. If you do this, then you are going to have issues getting the code to run.

When you are done testing out the code and you have gotten it all organized and ready to go, you must go back through and remove these comment characters. This helps you to turn the whole program back on so you can see if it works the right way.

Take a break from the code any time that it is needed

It is easy to really get into the code that you are writing, and you do not want to walk away and leave it. This is a great thing to have so much passion for the code that you are working with. However, if you are looking through all of the details for a long period of time, and the mistakes are not getting fixed and nothing seems to be working out the way that you want, then this can get even more frustrating.

When you get to this point, it is time to take a break. It is easy to want to keep working on the code and hope that it is going to get better for you. However, honestly, this is where your wheels are going to get stuck, and it is likely that you will just make the problem worse, while really bringing your frustration levels up to an all-time high.

Yes, you want to stick around and figure out the code and get it to work out for you. However, you are just going to get more and more lost and ruin the code. Taking a break and getting away from the code can make all of the difference. Whether it is just for a few hours or you take a few days off from the code that you are writing, you will find that giving your mind a break to recharge and try again later can make all of the difference in the world.

Working on coding in Python is intended to be simple and can aid you to write some powerful codes that work well. However, this does not mean there will not be times when you are working on some code and it just will not work the way that you want it to. Following some of the tips above and learning how to correct your own work along the way is going to make a difference and will ensure that you can correct some of the issues that show up in your code all on your own.

Conclusion

Thank you for making it through to the end of *Python Programming*, let us hope it was informative and able to provide you with all of the tools you need to achieve your goals whatever they may be.

The next step is to start seeing what you can do to make some of your own programs with the Python code. There is a lot to learn how to do with this somewhat coding, and hopefully, you have already downloaded the Python program, and all of its folders, and had a chance to work on some of the different codes that we discussed to gain some familiarity with how it works. This can give you a great start to working in Python, even if you have never done any coding in the past.

Many people are scared to get into the process of coding. They assume that they need to have a lot of experience to make this happen, or technical knowledge behind them to see the results. However, in reality, whether you have a lot of coding and computer experience, or you are brand new and just starting out, the Python code is going to be the right place to get started.

When you are ready to learn some of the basics that come with the Python language, and how you are able to use it to your advantage to create some of your own codes, even as a beginner, make sure to take a look at this guidebook to help you get started.

Finally, if you found this book useful in any way, a review on Amazon is always appreciated!

www.ingramcontent.com/pod-product-compliance
Lightning Source LLC
LaVergne TN
LVHW082036050326
832904LV00005B/203